•

"MORE IMPORTANT THAN THE WILL TO WIN,
IS THE WILL TO PREPARE."

CHARLY MUNGER

•

INTRODUCTION

I. BEFORE

MINDSET

1. From where you are, to filmmaker
2. The most important question is: Why?
3. The least important question is: How?
4. Go for meaning
5. Be a scientist

PRACTICAL ANALOGIES

1. Film as language
2. Film as a moving painting
3. Film as a service

II. DURING

STRATEGIES TO MAKE THINGS HAPPEN

1. Don't fund the movie, fund the execution of it
2. Look forward, plan backwards
3. Idea vs. Idea for a story
4. Brainstorm looking in the mirror
5. Quantity eventually finds quality

ON SET

1. Have rules (not laws)
2. Preparation allows focus
3. Experiment and go with the flow
4. Directing actors
5. Solving problems (because you'll have them).

MAKING "DOUBLE RIDDLE, WHAT COLOR DO YOU SEE?"

1. Story and Ideas
2. Writing the script
3. Building a team
4. Finding actors, or finding characters
5. Value-engineering the script
6. Editing & Tone
7. Sound and Music scoring
8. Color Correcting

III. AFTER

10 LESSONS LEARNED

ACKNOWLEDGEMENT

INTRODUCTION

I can't really tell if there are any great books about making movies, except for the only ones I ever read, Sydney Lumet's "Making Movies", and David Mamet's "On Directing Films". What I do know is that there are amazing movies you can learn a lot from by simply watching them carefully. Second to actually making them, watching movies is the best way to learn, and reading books would only be my third go to source for knowledge and inspiration.

Specially when it comes to directing, books can only validate what you already know directing is, or show you a way to direct that contrasts with your own instincts. They will not teach you how to be a good director. That will only happen at the job and then by seeing the results, good or bad. It's the same for making movies, you can't quite teach it, you can only share your way of doing it.

The only use of books on filmmaking is convincing oneself that others had the same fears and insecurities you may feel now, and see how those people went about it. To go even further, I would say that every book you read will help you make better movies, except the books about making movies.

With that in mind, in this book I try to give you insights of how I approached making my first film without film school and what I learned at each phase. These ideas are independent of technology, or style, or industry standard practices. After reading these pages, if you still think making a movie is the best way to spend your time, I hope you take away some practical ideas to be more efficient and intelligent than I was in the process, and also get better results.

If you stop reading here, take this with you: you have to put in the work first, be willing to go all the way, and expect nothing in return. You either have the obsession now, or maybe later, but you need to be obsessed with it, something nobody can teach you, and yet, the only way how your first movie will get made. So let's get to work.

I. BEFORE

MINDSET

1. FROM WHERE YOU ARE TO FILMMAKER

You are not a filmmaker until you make a movie, any movie, of any length. If you make a movie today, you are a filmmaker in the morning. That's not your problem, or a challenge of any kind.

I'd like to suggest that you should not care about conventions and titles, ever. You will do your film because you have come to the conclusion that you have no choice. It calls you from all directions and you must turn it into a reality. For me it happened very late in life. Filmmaking is my second career. And I entered it after three events happened in my life. I discovered video editing. I discovered Charlie Chaplin. And I discovered death. A skill, a role model and a wakeup call.

Editing images gave me a creative control that I never experienced drafting blueprints as an architect, which is what I had gone to school for and practiced for almost a decade; Charlie Chaplin showed me (didn't tell me) the possibilities of expressing ideas, opinions and stories with creativity, humor and simplicity. And the passing of my mother reminded me that I would die one day too, and that one should always try to do what one really wants. Life is brief.

Money and status aside, what adventure I wanted to live? I was an architect in Los Angeles, not bad at all, but the answer was, a filmmaker in New York City, or anywhere really, but I liked the idea of living in New York for a few years.

I must have watched Chaplin's Modern Times 50 times or so and I still couldn't believe that so many things could happen through one man's inspiration. I saw all the possibilities and disciplines I liked.

I still find architecture absolutely amazing but a few things in film were more exciting. For instance the unpredictability of film. You can't pull out a garden out of nowhere in the last week of construction of a building, but in movies, you can find a magic moment in the last minute of the last day in the editing room. The process is always discovering things that not even the filmmaker can predict. I couldn't see the same potential in architecture without major changes to the laws of physics or to the physics of laws.

Gravity and specially city building codes are too much of an obstacle to express ideas beyond form and function. Light on the other hand, is pretty much the only constant you can't do anything about, as in how it affects the human eye, but everything else is malleable in filmmaking.

I also found interesting the potential for more impact and less consequences. A bad building is something users and the city itself have to live with for years and years. Our cities are full of such buildings. A bad film simply disappears. Movies are powerful in their success and harmless in their failure. And finally, there was music, which I loved and could interact more with through film. All these thoughts, right or wrong, were some of the things I would think about at age 28 before I changed careers. And I knew I was starting 10 years late, so the way I saw it was that I was also starting 50 years early.

In the future, VR will allow architects be more like filmmakers and filmmakers be more like architects, making both disciplines more interesting perhaps.

I studied acting for about a year in workshops in Bogotá and Los Angeles. Studying acting I learned to understand the actors' journey, communicate with them and respect their crazy life choices. After all, Chaplin was a performer and I wanted to be him in some way. I studied all the great actors I could, their roles and their films (mostly American actors). Then after a few humiliating auditions I learned I didn't want to be an actor only (like most actors) and that I didn't have enough discipline to just act and do nothing else. I wanted to write and direct as well. Like, Chaplin.

During the next 6 years I learned editing, managed to make a living producing all kinds of videos, and studied on my own by watching films, until it was time to try to make my own. Big first mistake was waiting so long.

In the years leading to that moment, I had watched hundreds of films, a few of them several times, sometimes without sound, sometimes with different scores, sometimes muted. 2001 Space Odyssey to Pink Floyd's The Wall, or whatever combination you want to imagine. I had made a short film called Limbo during my Italian cinema period, just to mimic shots from Michelangello Antonioni and Vittorio Da Sica, and I had written one draft of a script for years, that turned into my way to study structure and characters, but nothing else happened.

I had to come up with a new idea, and a new script. Time went by and then one day I found myself in a short midlife crisis of sorts. I don't recommend this path to action but it was how it happened to me, and how I realized that the most important question to ask yourself, the one that will push you through all the storms ahead, is not so much how, but why. And if the why is strong, it will carry you.

•

"IF EVERYONE CAN DO IT THESE DAYS WITH
THE TECHNOLOGY AVAILABLE, WHY
SHOULD YOU DO IT? MAKE SURE THIS
PARTICULAR FILM YOU WILL MAKE ONLY
CAN BE MADE BY YOU… AND IF YOU THINK
SOMEONE CAN DO IT BETTER THAN YOU,
THEN DON'T DO IT."

WIM WENDERS

•

1. THE MOST IMPORTANT QUESTION IS: WHY?

Why you do things is more important than what you do. If you have enough good reasons for the things you do, your chances to succeed at them automatically increase. If it's important enough to you, you will not give up, and that's pretty much all it takes.

If you have that burning desire to make a film, because it is meant to be and nothing will stop you, please get me out of your way right now and do it, stop reading and begin to write. But if you are still thinking whether or not you have what it takes to make it happen, or you are not sure how to go about it, a good start is to ask yourself that simple question: why do I want to make a film? why *this* particular film?

It's not about having the right reason, but to be sure you are not operating from having the wrong reasons. If your reason is fun, and you are 16 years old or younger, do it. That's how Steven Spielberg, Christopher Nolan, David Fincher and many others began their careers between ages of 8 and 16. It's when you get older, that reasons become more important. If your reason is contribution to the world, do something else like feeding the poor, become a teacher or a plumber, these professions are more useful to society than filmmaking. If your reason is love of photography, music, stories, and exploring all aspects of our reality, that's more like, at least in my own experience. If your reason is fame, awards and money, you need to study more about life and less about Hollywood. Those things are good to aspire to as a byproduct of your work, perhaps as motivation of the rewards that come with intense work, but they shouldn't be the reasons for you to make movies.

"The question at the job is not what am I getting, the question is, what am I becoming?" (different authors have come up with different variations of this quote) but is one to keep in mind when you set a goal for yourself, specially one that will demand a lot of time and energy.

Who do you need to become to get the job done? Don't take that lightly. One could argue that the experience is enough good reason, if you are able to reflect on it and learn a few things. Making films is not a thing of gods or saints or genius, but it takes discipline, and to get hard things done with discipline is not a bad character treat to exercise.

Assuming that you will learn something, I want to increase your odds of success and not just have more "wisdom" at the end of the journey. You have to make a good film. And getting from "I made a movie", to "I made a good movie", there is a big damn gap you want to narrow as much as you can before you begin. As far as I am concerned, I couldn't make a good enough movie at the end of the day. But it wasn't the worst I've seen either, and that was better than a complete disaster. Or so I like to tell myself.

Charlie Munger, one of the most successful investors in America says that "what you think may change what you do, but perhaps most importantly, what you do may change what you think". So if you ask me what was the biggest gift I took from making a film, the answer is that doing it changed the way I thought about filmmaking, as a craft, a career, a calling, an industry, and it changed how I look at life in general. If you think about it, you will be making some sacrifices, committing to finish a difficult task, maintaining sanity while you do it, and solving problems at every step of the way. That is a good adventure to have and one from which you will be forced to learn something no matter what, therefore changing your perspective on things.

Your reasons will be yours only, all I can recommend is that they are strong so you can finish what you start.

Wim Wenders said it best, "If everyone can do it these days with the technology available, why should you do it? Make sure this particular film you will make only can be made by you. That no one could tell that particular story better than you, and if you think someone can do it better than you, then don't do it."

•

"THE ONLY SAFE THING IS TO TAKE A CHANCE"

MIKE NICHOLS

•

2. THE LEAST IMPORTANT QUESTION IS: HOW?

We can both hear that voice in your mind asking: How do I make this movie? Or, How do I make any movie? I'm here to tell you that the answer can only be found after you make it, and that happens one small step at a time.

It reminds me of a quote I read - supposedly from Francis Ford Coppola – that said something like this: "…a movie is a little like a question, you only get the answer when you make it."

Take what you wish from that, yet I still believe that there is no major mystery, only to prepare as best as you can, and simply having the grit to not stop moving forward. So pull the trigger and don't wait for a perfect idea.

Some people will not write anything until they have the money. They won't write a script until they are happy with some treatment. They won't find actors until they are satisfied with the script. They won't read this book until they have the script funded. And they think they can't fund it because they don't have the right actors attached to the project. I think that unless you jump, you can stay trapped in that circle forever. So, prepare for the jump, but then jump.

Go with an imperfect idea, write an imperfect treatment, an imperfect script, with imperfect actors, locations, equipment, budget, etc. You will train your intuition, your instincts, your innate taste and your ability to tell stories.

In the best case scenario, you have a picture (or many pictures) of the movie you want to make in your minds' eye and all you need to do is write a description of it on paper so that you can go with a team of people and capture that description in moving images. Then you put it all together and you have a movie.

However, on your first film (arguably in all films, but I can't be sure of that yet) things will take a different course, and that clear picture in your head may not be so defined, therefore you begin to question your ability to get the job done from the very beginning, when you shouldn't.

Preparation doesn't mean you need to have all the answers ahead of time. It means that at least you try to think about all the possible questions that could come up and make sure all the basics are covered. Your job is to prepare so well that whatever you have in your head is as clear as possible, then described as well as it possibly can, and then plan so it can be executed as closely to that vision as possible. If you do that, you can move forward no matter how many doubts you have, and you will find the rest of the answers as you go.

Each director has his or her own notion of what getting prepared includes. Due to experience and instinct some can capture the right material without storyboarding for example. Directors like Werner Herzog are against storyboards all together, "storyboards are for cowards", he says. And others with all the preparation, talent and instincts, can fail at getting what they need, or have a hard time putting it together.

Take Martin Scorsese's The Departed. I'm sure Scorsese did not have in his mind the fully completed picture as it ended up being. He has publicly talked about how difficult it was to put the story together so that it would work in all aspects. Of course when you have 50 years or so of experience and Thelma Shoonmaker as your editing partner, eventually you make it work. And they did.

And since you are not Herzog, or have made all the films Scorsese had made before The Departed, you should prepare.

In my view, the model to aspire to in your first feature would be more like The Cohen Brothers and the making of Blood Simple, one of the best suspense thrillers of independent cinema. I think for the most part the reason for its success (in time) was the fact that every single shot was storyboarded, and the whole piece was true to what the Cohen's wanted to make. They had an idea in their mind of each shot, how they would work together and what the result had to look like. In some cases a shot had to be exact to the millimeter, to cut with the following shot the way they wanted. That kind of preparation is something their star actress then, Frances McDormand, still talks about as being key to their success. With enough things figured out ahead of time, you can only make it better in the editing room.

Yet another practical reason for going in that direction is simply that if you want people to trust you with their money or talents, without you ever having made a movie before, you have to put in the work first and use your script and storyboards as a sort of guarantee that you mean business. And actors will believe that you know what you are doing, even when you don't.

Prepare as much as you can, not to the point of not taking action, but as much as you can nonetheless, and then go on the discovery journey as you please.

A good analogy is how actors can excel at improvisation. You can only do good improv if you know the original material or subject of conversation and roles forwards and backwards. Preparation.

Another reason is economy. You will spend money and most importantly time that you will never get back. And perhaps even more important, your reputation will begin to build on this first film, how well prepared you are, your clarity of vision and your respect for the time and efforts others will put in the making of your film. That's something not to take lightly either.

Even after all this preparation, things will change some. Form the moment you put pencil to paper until you do your last export (the one labeled "FINAL-this time for real-Rev-Z89.mov"), the film will morph and change in unexpected ways. Understanding this sort of natural tendency for things not to go as planned is a good thing to remember and learn to collaborate with.

Protect the initial concept. Everything else will fight to survive in service of that one concept and the story. Each part will change in relation to all the other parts, and in that sense, as a living organism, you have to trust that things will find their right place. I know it sounds a little too ethereal, but some things in life work that way.

Michael Jackson used to say that his advice to musicians was to get out of the way of the music. I would say, once you've written the script and prepared, get out of the way of the story that is there already and just help it come through when it gets stuck.

Then there is the element of time. You won't have all the time you would want, but I think speed also helps in the context of your first film. Working fast, you have no choice but to go with your gut, and at the end of the process it will be very clear which were your strengths and which were your weaknesses. Did you have a good sense of structure when you wrote, or did it all changed in the editing room? Did the characters come alive with your rapid casting selection, or did you miss the mark? Did the camera positioning worked in the context of editing sequences? Did your ideas fit what your tools were? Did your technique fit the story? Or didn't it? Where you able to maintain a motivated, focused and well fed team working for you for 10 or so consecutive days? All these basic parts of making a film you will get to experience on your first film under pressure, except the multi-million dollar pressure of your second film. It's a good opportunity.

So what you need to take away from all this is that you need not to worry about how things will unravel; the process will put your talent and skills to test and make you better and stronger. Just prepare and don't get paralyzed when you know you don't have all the answers ahead of time. The sooner you make a first film, the sooner you will make a second one. We are all going to die, so just fucking do it.

4. GO FOR MEANING.

Some people cry, others run, others write, others have kids, others travel, and others make films. That's how we cope with life and reality, or how we escape from it. Doing what we love.

A way to check your reasons to make your film is to look for meaning. When things mean the world to you, It will make you push the boulder all the way up to the top of the hill even when you feel your arms can't push anymore.

When I say meaning it applies in four different ways. One is what making films means to you; second, the meaning of the films you make, and the one you are about to work on in particular. Third is the meaning of the pictures you put on your film. And fourth the meaning of the stories and what the characters say. This is just for you to know, not the public. All you need to remember is that meaning, my opinion, is the ultimate compass.

In a more pragmatic context, Stanley Kubrick said in an interview, talking about advertising that "If someone could transfer what advertisers do in 30 seconds of a TV ad to a feature film, it would be something remarkable". And what he meant I think, was that advertisers use images in such an effective and efficient way, that every frame means something and communicates something to the audience, ultimately conveying and "selling" you on an idea, concept, or product in just 30 seconds. That is how much power images and montage have, on the surface and also at a subconscious level. It depends on your education and skill to exploit that power and serve the story in the best way you can. Kubrick also comments that movies should be looked at more as works of art than pure entertainment, and I think this too has to do with meaning. Every frame matters.

One experiment to understand how each image affects the meaning of the whole, is the one by Alfred Hitchcock, when explaining montage. Hitchcock took 3 images and changed the one in the middle, completely transforming the meaning of the entire piece when the 3 images were projected as a sequence. First, close-up of an old man focused looking at something. Then, a medium shot of a woman with her baby. And lastly, back to the close-up of the man, who now slowly smiles.

Then, he replaced the woman with the baby piece, with the image of a young woman in a small bikini. Just with that change, the sequence goes from a benevolent grandfather figure that smiles out of love looking at his daughter and grandchild, to a dirty old man that smiles when looking at a random young girl in a bikini. This example of course was made over 50 years ago, but you get the point. Every frame has in theory the same power than all the other frames. Frames to a sequence are like words to a sentence.

If you can tell by now, the levels of depth that you can play with on film, are just as numerous as you let your knowledge and imagination produce. So be curious about the meaning of things and learn as much as you can about all things, and hopefully with a sense of humility, always remember that we know nothing.

5. BE A SCIENTIST

I believe you learn the most from experimentation. You try things, you break them up, re-build them and from that you get better understanding of how they work to begin with. Using that mentality in the context of your first film is a good way to discover things you can't come up with in any other way. You demystify the complexities of making films because once you can look at the parts, you get a hold of how things get made no matter how intimidating they look like to an audience. A simple way to do this is to watch one of your favorite films again and reverse engineer.

At the time I was beginning to write my first script, I used Martin Scorsese's Taxi Driver and Quentin Tarantino's Pulp Fiction. I also used The Shinning by Stanley Kubrick, and Last Tango in Paris by Bernardo Bertolucci. I would watch these films and start timing the beginning and the end of each scene. Then I would watch each scene and count the number of shots per scene. Then I would see what kind of shots went in on each sequence, who was on the shot, and how long each shot was. It was almost like creating a shot list and a storyboard from watching the film. Not completely but good chunks of it.

If you are new to filmmaking and you are not making films from age 8, this is a great way to learn about filmmaking. Do this with just one movie (hopefully a good one) and you will be way ahead of the game. It's like figuring out how to play a song just by listening to it over and over again until you figure out every chord with your own guitar.

I reversed engineer some of my favorite movies. Pulp Fiction, Reservoir Dogs, The Shining, Blood Simple, Vertigo, The Bicycle Thieve, 2001, Modern Times, and others. Unfortunately not all with the same level of detail, and perhaps that's one of many reasons I couldn't make a good picture yet.

You must keep doing it until you begin to find gafs, continuity issues, room tone changes, and weird adlib. When you find a strange cut on a Hitchcock film, weird continuity "issues" on Scorsese's films or Kubrick then you know you've been paying some attention to detail, and even better, you can humanize these directors and realize it's all about craftsmanship and the effect of the parts in relation to the whole, and rarely of the individual images alone. This is why some movies can look beautiful frame by frame, and still have no effect to an audience.

Don't underestimate repetition. Watching the same film 10 times or a hundred is flexing your directorial muscles. That's why directors talk about watching one thousand films before they started making their first film, and why it allowed them to be good at it. When you dissect and reverse engineer films, is like you are making the film in your mind, and to a limited extent, your brain can't tell the difference between studying and actually making it, which should bring you some joy. If you don't feel compelled enough to dissect your favorite films, filmmaking may not be as close to your heart as it needs to be. It's that kind of obsession.

Another exercise is watching films without sound, or to the score of other films. This exercise is not only fun but you discover connections and reasons of why the score is what it is, the impact of music in storytelling, and if they are in general good films at all without the music crutch.

Watch silent films. Watch them asking yourself constantly why what you are watching makes sense to the story, why are you watching it and what is keeping you entertained. Why is it that even without dialogue the story still works and moves you. Whether you are a Buster Keaton or a Charlie Chaplin fan, watch them both, and others. Do all these things and more, do you own experiments. Be a scientist.

PRACTICAL ANALOGIES

1. FILM AS LANGUAGE

Humans communicate mainly through speech and body language. Mostly body language, and that's why what we see an actor do is so powerful and more important than what they say. Our ability to turn images into meaning and link meanings to build stories in our heads is nothing more than a very sophisticated but also primitive kind of language.

Film is a language, and as such, it's in constant evolution.

I remember looking at some of the Egyptian hieroglyphs one time, with human figures walking (or rather standing sideways), with objects in the sky, animals carrying human heads and so on; and I thought that perhaps all these sceneries had nothing to do with what the Egyptians were like or about the things that were normal to their civilization. Consider that our civilization is wiped out and a new one came and found our films and nothing else as a testament of our existence. They find Star Wars, The Shape of Water and Jurassic Park. Would that be proof of our reality or our society? The answer of course is no, it would only be testimony of our imagination. So likely when someone think they find a flying object on an ancient tablet and claim aliens came to visit earth, I think we are just seeing art. They didn't know what to do with light and film, but they knew how to use chisels and stone. They could have had their own version of science fiction, fantasy and drama expressed by carving their thoughts into stone.

The point is that if you understand the depth that is behind a piece of film you can enjoy it more when you study and when you make it. In fact, I believe, that whenever you come up to a dead end, knowing the existence of these layers will give you more ways to find a solution to your problem, or in some cases, realize that there is no problem to begin with.

You often hear someone who speaks a new language say: I can understand some, and I can read it, but I can't speak it. It's the same with film. Most people can understand them to an extent, some can push a button and capture videos, but only a few can speak it fluently and eloquently. If you have a great vocabulary, and master grammar, you can do visual poetry; and while you may come up with a film nobody understands, the work, the story and the meaning is still there.

There is no right or wrong, but one thing is for sure, if all you know is 10 words and just one way to use them in a sentence, you want to expand your knowledge as much as possible as quick as possible before you put pen to paper, and light to film. And then possibilities become infinite.

2. FILM AS A MOVING PAINTING

A painting is another analogy I like to use. Except, your painting changes 24 times per second, and you decide how, when and where each frame fits in the picture, at each second, within that universe you created.

If you listen carefully to masters of the craft like Hitchcock, or Guillermo del Toro, understanding deeply this aspect is what differentiates their work from any other. They are not just telling a story. The whole film is one big 4 dimensional painting made with very fine strokes.

Once you understand and look at films in this way, you can begin to understand why some movies are masterpieces, and others are just movies with very short life, like a painting that never makes it out of the easel, or if it does, one that is quickly forgotten even by its author. Ideas, meaning, light, composition, colors, technique, materials, tools, dialogue, etc. it all matters, and the more you know, the better.

This analogy is also useful when you get too caught up in what the industry wants, or how your film would play in festivals. You can't ask a painter to work thinking about the museum's selection criteria. Every time someone would say something to the effect of "too long for a short, too short for a feature" I ask myself what does that even mean? would you tell a painter that they must use one specific canvas size just to get into a museum? Make the film and your story as long or as short as it needs to be and the way you think it should be. Don't worry about the rest of it, or at least don't make any of the industry common practices dictate your artistic decisions. Filmmaking is an art form, always beware of "rules".

1. FILM AS A SERVICE

But what kind of art form? I believe one of the biggest misconceptions one can be confused by when making films is that it has some kind of special status, even as an art form, or by the same token, that it is useless because it's art.

While one could argue that a great piece of filmmaking is of more value to society at large than a great meal at a restaurant, if we try to put them in the same basket, by principle, they are two different kinds of food. One is food for your stomach, the other for your brain. Someone will use their time to consume what you make, and you don't want to give them anything but your best to consume. You will want to take someone's mind on an exciting visual and / or emotional journey.

This has nothing to do with having a moral take on what you produce. Violence, sex or faulty language, has nothing to do with it. But I do think that quality thinking matters. Be obsessed with the quality of your work. In times when we all ask for more, better and faster; in times of too much information, quality is the only thing that is worth being known for.

When you think of filmmaking as a service, it helps you stay in touch with reality. Your work is not just a service to an audience, but also a service to the writers, the actors, the crew, and everyone else who put time into it. Finishing the best film you can is good for all of those involved. And as a bonus, it feels better to see the film as a something larger than yourself.

And if none of these analogies click in your head, go with this: just make something beautiful. That alone is hard enough, and it services everyone.

•

MAKE IT HAPPEN.

•

II. DURING

STRATEGIES TO MAKE THINGS HAPPEN

1. DON'T FUND THE MOVIE, FUND THE EXECUTION OF IT

If you look at it very closely, the word "money" has the same letters as "lazy". Or maybe it doesn't, but you get the idea.

Money is probably the #1 excuse why people don't do things. Before I share my philosophy I will say I did spent some money and mostly sweat equity money. But having the first 6K with which I began, was not the reason why or how I was able to pull it off.

It's not the money that will make the film happen. Making the film will equip you with reasons to attract the money you need to finish it. Making the film comes first, at least on this first adventure.

Share your vision, and people will help you because you have that vision. They will buy into your project because you have the drive and nothing beats that when your wallet doesn't have enough cash to fund the project. Will this enthusiasm be enough? Not quite. But you have to have it. Someone said that when you move towards your target with determination, people tend to get out of your way, or help you achieve it.

Here's how far you can go with zero dollars:

• Come up with ideas or concepts. And pick one.

• Make a treatment (describe what is this film is about and how it looks like).

• Structure your story, beginning, middle and end.

• Write down the story as a tale.

• Describe your characters.

• Figure out what are the scenes needed to tell that tale.

• Meet actors at a café, or at a friend's place or wherever you can, actors will go where the work is.

• Make a shot list of your drafted script.

• Calculate how many days you need. Calculate costs.

• Figure out if you can do it all in one location or within the same block. List all the places you could use for free.

• Take pictures of those places you could use, imagine the scenes happening, block them out in your mind. Draw a sketch.

• Shoot one scene with your phone, edit it, and get a feel for the tone you are after and what the actors have to offer. Re-write. Read what you are writing with somebody else and listen to it, edit your dialogues.

• Find and listen to music that goes with your story, either for its tone, or lyrics, or as a score. File it.

• Sit down quietly or go for a walk, and write down your ideas. David Lynch says, if you can collect 70 ideas, you have a movie.

Your movie is practically finished. And you spent zero dollars.

But don't believe me. I have very little experience. Hitchcock used to say that he didn't like going to shoot the picture, because it was already done on paper. Shooting was just executing. Quentin Tarantino says, that he likes to have a script so good that if he didn't shoot it, he would be just as happy with the result of what's on the page. This my friends, takes zero dollars. Easier said than done, but it's the bloody truth, whether we like it or not.

Now you tell your friends and show them the script. Pull out some images of books, or other movies or your own sketches; wow them with what you are thinking about. Nobody knows if it's good or not, but it's there, printed and bind*. (there goes the first $20 bucks).

Maybe you can come up with a powerful visual for the story you want to tell. You pick up a book with a picture of the largest boat ever built, sinking in the ocean and say to your investors: "Romeo and Juliet, in that boat." Done. That was how James Cameron pitched the making of Titanic to the studios. This visual is so clear that the movie is there, you can write the words, do storyboards, all without a penny, and then it becomes a matter of executing your vision.

Then you realize nobody helped you. What do you do? You keep going and keep knocking on doors.

You ask your actors and some crew if they would do it for X amount. You make a fundraising campaign with family and friends, and hopefully this will encourage a couple more people to do the same.

You can also tell your lead actors this is for them as well, and see if they can contribute. This is something I didn't quite practiced, but I believe it makes sense. Your actors will build their careers as much as you will with the project. Do it together.

Be ready to shoot with your phone and play all characters if it's necessary. Hopefully this will not be the case, and I'm not advocating for such desperate measures, but that's how committed you need to be in your mind about making this happen.

Bills? You go to school or have a job? Make a stop in your social life for one month, or ayear. Work on your film at night until you pass out, and do it every day until the task is finished. Move back to your parents or a friend for a month and get it done. Nolan, Tarantino, they both shot films (Following, and My Best Friend's Birthday) on weekends a few hundred dollars at a time. You can do it too.

2. LOOK FORWARD, PLAN BACKWARDS

Take a piece of paper. What day is today? Take a calendar and decide when you want this movie to be completed. Be aggressive. It must happen this year. Pick a date and work backwards.

This is a quote I literally wrote down and put in front of my keyboard. "Think forward, plan backwards". If you have some experience producing any type of video, which you probably do, you can estimate how much time you will need to produce your movie, and if you don't, I hope this guide gets you started.

My calendar was built more or less in the following way. You are probably less reckless and will do better planning and better thinking.

• December 24th. Rough cut completed.

What does that mean? (I would ask myself)

It means that if I spend an average of 1 day editing 1 minute of film (consider, re edits, sound, color, etc), and my film is 70 minutes long, I must have completed shooting by:

• October 15th Finish shooting.

What does that mean?

It means that if I can film an average of 7 minutes of story per day, I need 10 days of filming. So I should start shooting on:

• October 5th First day of shooting.

What does that mean?

It means I will need to be all ready and coordinated 24 hours before I shoot. That day will probably be for handling last minute emergencies and charging batteries (literally and figuratively).

What does that coordination includes?

• 1 day to coordinate wardrobe
• 1 day to have a plan for food
• 1 day to coordinate/buy props
• 1 day to rent gear
• 1 day to work through your shot list.
• 1 day to meet up with your assistant director.
• 1 day to visit locations with your DP (if it's not you)
• 1 day for printing scripts, sides, shot lists, storyboards, etc.
• 1 day for unexpected bullshit.

That means that you have to be fully dedicated to preparing the first day of shooting by:

• September 25th Pre-production coordination.

What does that mean?

It means that by September 25th you must have finished casting, secured locations and confirmed the crew.

1 week to find and work with actors
1 week to find and recruit crew members.

It means that you should "stop writing" by:

• September 13th Script finished and storyboarded.

When I got to that conclusive date I looked at the calendar. It said: September 10st.

I had 3 days to come up with an idea and write until a script was finished. I wrote for a few days non-stop until I had 60 bad pages written down.

When things looked bad on the page, I kept writing. It was about quantity. I figured, and it was true, I would re-write anyways everyday, here and there, until the last day of post-production.

If you think you've had a tough boss in the past, you must be 10 times tougher on yourself, if you don't have discipline, it won't happen.

•

"AN IDEA FOR A STORY IS NOTHING BUT A MOMENT OR SITUATION YOU CAN SEE IN YOUR MINDS' EYE. THE STORY IS THE PROJECTION OF THAT IDEA IN TIME. IT'S UNFOLDING THAT IDEA TOWARDS THE FUTURE, THE PAST, OR BOTH."

•

3. IDEA VS IDEA FOR A STORY

We all know ideas come easy, the problem is getting good ones and then be able take action on a single one.

I would like to suggest that to think that you need "an idea" for a film is an overwhelming statement that can turn into a trap. Thinking about ideas makes me think that I need a 90 minute idea. Try to think about it in a different way.

You don't need an idea to make your first film. You need an idea for a story. And an idea for a story is nothing but a moment or situation you can visualize in your mind's eye. And the story is the projection of that idea in time. It's unfolding that idea towards the future or the past, or both.

If you go from there and begin to think about interesting moments, you will find much more fertile ground. A moment that fascinates you can fill hundreds of pages. And it will.
Imagine this situation: a guy dies in an elevator because it got stuck during a thanksgiving weekend at the office, and he didn't survive the three days. That's an idea for a story based on a situation. It's that dramatic picture of a moment or situation that

can be very clear in your head, and then you can unfold it in a million different ways. It's not the greatest example, but you get the point.

Quentin Tarantino said once "if you love cinema enough, you can't help but making a good film". Easy for him to say, but what I find interesting and true about that, is that it is more effective to focus on loving the craft and the process, than spending your energy in search of a particular story or the perfect idea. At least on your first film this is definitely true.

Keep in mind that from one story to another, your talent and the quality of your execution will still show, so your story is important but almost any decent story will take you from point A to point B, and test your skills in the process.

4. BRAINSTORM LOOKING IN THE MIRROR

Films don't have to be an autobiography, but your own human experience and thoughts are material that should be used, and you have that already. And I also don't mean literally, you can make an 80 year old monk on a wheelchair get lost in Brooklyn and through him explore the feelings you experienced in your own life. Whatever is in your life is material to add meaning to new ideas and situations.

Now, that is a conclusion I came about, but not exactly what I did at the beginning. To warm up, I decided to write down 5 or so short ideas for stories. I wrote them as a summary a newspaper would write of each to sell tickets or something. And since you will need those anyways, you can again look forward and plan backwards. What would be a summary of your film?

These are a couple dumb ones I came up with in a few hours:

• American Temptation (Action-Drama)
In the last day of a vacation trip, blinded by shiny NYC, a couple will get an unexpected offer: 1 million dollars if they deliver a suspicious envelope to a man waiting down the street. Tempted by a prosperous and brighter future for their soon to be born child, the challenge will unleash a chain of events that will draw a very dark present, in which they may loose everything they already have. Destiny is one block away.

• Bloody Honeymoon (Crime-Action-Thriller)
Posing as a couple in their honey moon, a man and a woman are sent for one last criminal job to NYC: deliver a small case with a mysterious cyber-drug. Half way through the job, tempted, they try the drug

and discover a new and powerful parallel reality. Having decided to abort the mission, sell the goods in the bag and escape. They are now on the run with an undelivered package, their crime organization and their associates are after them. An overdose might be their way to salvation, or their self-inflicted death sentence.

• Deleted (Sci-fi-Thriller)
A scientist is about to release a study that proves that we live in a non-real world. The night before his first official presentation, he receives a visit from a government's secret agent. If he doesn't stop, he will be "erased", which now he knows is possible. Later that night, when his wife shows up she does not recognize him and there seems to be no way now to prove his identity.

• Dinner 2100 (Sci-Fi)
Year 2100. Freedom of speech and privacy are things from the past. What you say is recorded and processed in real time. Some words and ideas should not be mentioned out loud. When one of three friends uses the wrong words to describe recent political events while having dinner, it will compromise the safety of the whole group by association. In a matter of minutes two government agents show up. One will face a death penalty on the spot, unless they can turn the agents against each other.

• Virtual Assassin (Action-Sci-Fi-Drama)
On his 10th year anniversary, a man gets unfairly fired from his job. Unemployed, he is hooked by a new drug; a pill that can transport him to virtual realities. When he discovers that he can affect real life in this virtual world, he will try to take revenge of his former boss through it, but he could get lost in the attempt.

Above are examples of premises for stories, some bad and some less bad. Who knows, but the point is you will begin to find places or themes of interest unique to you. In my case it was always some mystery, duality, relationships with technology and some kind of man vs. system themes. Somewhere there I think there is the immigrant or traveler's mind. Nothing too original, but they were all things I could work with because I want to know more about those topics myself. And all had some autobiographical aspect in disguise. Likely my second film will come up from that list.

Come up with your own absurd ideas, things you understand or want to understand. One of the reasons you are a filmmaker is that you have a point of view of things, situations or life at large you want to explore, learn more about and in some ways surrender to, precisely because you do not understand them.

Now that you have a few concepts written down, get some feedback. Share and see how others react to each story. This is not for getting approval of your ideas but to test the clarity of your own thinking.

I shared my ideas with 6 people and 4 of them had a different favorite story that they liked, but the exercise helped me put some ideas out of my head and not get stuck. The final result, what would become "Double Riddle, What Color Do You See?" had ingredients of all of them in one way or another.

I tried different combinations and mixed storylines. And then came the secret sauce, best said by the great director James Gray: "The closer you can get to being personal, the better the work is."

I believe this to be a crucial aspect of art and cinema. The work will be better if you can find elements of the film that are close to you personally. As I said, I don't think a film has to be autobiographical at all, but people who know you must be able to see you through it, in some way. If that is not there, I think you are leaving half of your value on the table, the good half to be more precise.

Even on a film like Star Wars, seemingly fantasy and science fiction, or adaptations of books such as The Clockwork Orange, I think a director finds his or her way into the material. I can't tell what it was for George Lucas and Stanley Kubrick, but I will speculate that for Lucas it was a whole theory of life and the fight between good and evil, and the relationship father son; and for Kubrick, ideas that went with his own view of society and his relationship with authority at the time.

Adding that personal element will add meaning to your work, so that you don't desist when things get difficult. The film will follow you for the rest of your life, or at least for a couple of years and I think you should feel good about it today and hopefully also in the future. You can also be Roger Corman and be a doer. God bless his contribution to so many careers, maybe that was the meaningful thing to him.

How I found the story for Double Riddle was "easy". I had those ingredients I wanted to explore mentioned before, and I was coming out of a painful breakup. I had to put that in. But what kept me interested in the project was exploring the mystery and the surveillance and paranoid journey of the character. Was everything in the film true? of course not. But it was relatable enough for me to understand what the characters where doing. I think at the end was a very superficial exercise, not cinematic enough, but you will do better.

Quentin Tarantino mentioned this at an interview with Charlie Rose. About the fact that if you are not letting your life and current mental state affect your writing (or your performance for that matter) your job is not quite where it should be. And in that line of thought, let's remember QT first film, the never released "My Best Friend's Birthday". What can be more familiar and personal than that?

Another feeling I went through that you might also encounter is that no idea seems special or unique enough. Don't be afraid to tell a story that has been told before. It's your first film and what the focus must be on is on finishing the damn thing no matter what and learn as much as possible. Stories get repeated through time over and over again. If you look into psychology, history and literature, you will find this is part of who we are. Our myths and legends are but a few and we only change some superficial aspects of them and make them our own. Remember Titanic? It's an original take on an exciting love story that has always existed. Why not?

And If you are stuck with many ideas, look around you and eliminate by looking at what you can actually use. You live with two roommates, they will let you shoot over a weekend. You own a bicycle, your favorite period of history is ancient Egypt, your favorite film is David Fincher's Fight Club and you had a fight with one of your parents and the wound is open. How could you turn that into a story? Play with that.

An archeology student has a fight with his father and goes on biking around town, piking up fights just to demonstrate he is strong and courageous, something his father, who's a retired failed boxer can't admit.

Maybe your film has to be about a guy (or a girl) who's trying to decode the meaning of the Giza Pyramid (because you already have a bunch of books and posters in your room about it). Who knows. Do not underestimate the value of free props and "art-ready" sets. It will bring more truth to your story.

Not satisfied? Some of the most successful directors began by doing exactly that. We mentioned Christopher Nolan in Following, Quentin Tarantino in My best Friend's Birthday, and we can also include Richard Linklater's "It's Impossible to Learn to Plow by Reading Books". Stanley Kubrick used his NY Apartment to shoot "Eyes Wide Shot" at the end of his career, why wouldn't you use what you have at the beginning?

Be creative and resourceful, is one of the main skills you must develop. Two more examples to inspire you could be "My Dinner With Andre" by Louis Malle, and "Tape" also by Richard Linklater as well, pretty much one-location movies. And by the end of each one of those films the last thing you are thinking is the fact that it all happened in one room. So in other words, you have all you need. Don't agonize anymore. Like Alfred Hitchcock said: "It's just a movie". (He also said he was never really able to convince himself of that).

As you brainstorm for stories, think about structure. Luc Godard used to say that a film must have a beginning, a middle and an end, but not necessarily in that order. David Mamet responded: "that's why those films are so bad". There is no right way or wrong way to go about finding a structure to your story. But there are a few things you may want to think about, play with and do consciously because it is an important aspect of filmmaking and storytelling, and like the word says, it is a structure. A building collapses without a structure, and so do stories.

I used one main book to just get me going about structure. The Hero's Journey by Joseph Campbell. If you are a film student you were probably instructed to read it, if you are new to the craft, grab it, and read it. Speed-read if you need to, and think about how the principles of structure apply to your story and your characters. And if you have an idea of the rules, then you can break them and do things your way.

Make a map of the story, with boxes and arrows and notes. Where the story begins, what happens after, what happens next, and so on. See how that affects the whole thing, what your characters do about it, how they overcome the obstacles, and how the story ends. This is a useful way to play with structure, because you can see the story as a machine with parts that are related to each other to find an ultimate effect.

Another film to study is "El Mariachi", by Robert Rodriguez. Famous for being a film made with $7,000 dollars by a 23 year old, but what I think it should really be famous for, is for being a very good film. Watch it, break it apart, find the structure and the story and the character's journey. Steal all the good ideas and put them to test in your own draft asking yourself how you are going about the same problems of structure, character, dialogue, and so on. Study Christopher Nolan's "Memento", QT's "Reservoir Dogs", Luis Buñuel's "Un Chien Andalou", and Chris Maker's "La Jetée". Chew on that in terms of structure.

Once you have that "events map" clear on paper with the main moments that make the story be a story, get ready to sit your ass down and start writing until you can see this page number at the bottom: page 70.

So there you have it: Look in the mirror of your life, use what you have, write even when it's bad, use your passions, throw all ideas to paper, and give them some structure. Don't stop writing, sometimes quantity   is   the   way   to   quality.

5. QUANTITY EVENTUALLY FINDS QUALITY

If you have a piece of software like Final Draft, that is great. But if you don't, just use a word processor. If you don't have a computer, do it by hand. All you need to know is that there are some conventions in scriptwriting, and tools available to format your script in the right ways, and you can do that later. Right now it's about quantity of ideas and pages, not the format.

Here is your first big obstacle. Can you sit down and just write until you get the page count you need? This is when your skill of "commitment to the task at hand" is necessary. Diligence, discipline and focus.

It's really all it takes… It worked for me, and I'm not a very disciplined, focused person. I'm also not a gifted writer, and English is my second language. I can be diligent, but that's hardly enough. I had a piece of paper next to my desk that said something like "write 60 pages", and underneath said something like "start auditions". It was that simple, I had to write 60 pages of whatever came to mind so I could keep moving ahead, and I had 3 days to do it, or something like that.

Here is a key aspect to consider (in my opinion), to be able to write a page that will not be completely useless at the end of the day.

On every page, at the top type this question: what happened here? Did the story move forward or stayed the same? Is this page making me want to know what happens next? Every page should move your film forward, in some way. And if dialogue is all you have, look for opportunities to show who these characters are, instead of using them simply as vehicles of information and dialogue. Can they be doing something specific that conveys information?. Of course doing nothing in the middle of a desert is also something. But for example, if a character is sharpening a knife while the phone speaker has an on hold annoying music, and he is looking at the speaker, I'm sticking around. If instead he is having a verbal fight over the phone with costumer support, screaming his complaint, maybe not. In both cases, he is a very unhappy costumer. Isn't he?

Analyze films from that place. The first few lines in "Blood Simple" are right away very specific to the situation that is about to unfold, a woman will cheat her husband with their marriage counselor. And think about, what if this couple had been talking about hamburgers in Amsterdam like in Pulp Fiction; would it be the same? Or what if their initial conversation had taken place at a park bench on a Sunday afternoon instead of the car and in the middle of a dark road? Play with those different combinations in your head. There is no correct answer but I believe you should think and be aware about these different ways to make stories unfold visually. Use what Andrew Carnegie called synthetic imagination, a very useful creative tool.

In any case, don't stop writing at page 5 or 10, really push yourself to get the count of pages you need, and then begin to sculpt each page. There is always a key called delete.

●

"THE MOST DIFFICULT AND CHALLENGING
THING ABOUT DIRECTING A FILM, IS
GETTING OUT OF THE CAR"

STEVEN SPILBERG

●

ON SET

1. HAVE RULES (NOT LAWS)

Hopefully by the time you are on set, you are not consciously thinking about all the details that will need to be figured out and every small decision. You are simply on automatic, troubleshooting. What I mean by that is that if you are focused and have done your planning, you will be doing one of two things or both. Executing the plan or solving problems that somehow impede execution.

A good word of encouragement goes a long way at the beginning. Nobody is getting time back into their lives and the only thing that makes sense to do is the best job we can. I think I said something about being there to learn, make a movie, and have a good time and while I did that only once at the very beginning of shooting, it set the tone of "my" set.

If you are paying people, as you should in one way or another, cut cellphones or whatever technology gadgets that are a distraction. I didn't make it a must, but when someone was checking their phone, one look would put it right back in their pockets. I believe any distraction from anyone takes away from the best result possible. The way I see it, each person on set is driving a car, fast, on a narrow road, in the dark, with a thousand feet high fall on each side, and another crew member is following them. If someone gets distracted, the car goes off the road, and whoever is behind will inevitably follow. Remind everyone how important their job is in order for the project to succeed. Being efficient could mean you got to shoot that extra take where everyone nailed it for the first time or something special happened and made the film better.

Respect on set is also of first order. It begins with you and your AD. I tend to be easy on people because my priority is to move forward, a simple – let's not do that – will fix almost anything permanently when you work with smart people.

I found that as long as people see you working as hard as you can, they will go along. Even when the stakes are high, the stomach is empty, it's raining outside and you can't figure out the best way to shoot what's in front of you. Sounds stupid as I write these things down, but a good atmosphere and good service to your team could prevent homicidal thoughts on take 35.

Don't underestimate logistics for a second. Know where things will go and who will be responsible. Anticipate where gear, bags and trash go, where the tape will be, the flashlight, a screwdriver, a hammer, plastic bags, all these things really help. A set where you know where everything is and who is in charge of what means you have an army and a strategy to win the battle. If there is no such planning there is chaos.

Where will the props be, and who will take charge. Know where people can hang their coats and where actors can change and keep their suitcase with all the wardrobe options you asked for them to bring. Where can they have a moment of solitude and silence. Chaos will happen, just minimize it (this is another strategy you can use in general, minimizing all thinkable blind spots and deal only with real surprises).

Between "it's a wrap" at night and "action" the next morning, you will need to keep working. You will be downloading footage from the day (into that folder structure you created ahead of time, labeled and organized appropriately on your computer). You may be taking a look at the footage at random in case something calls your attention (too dark, blown out, or anything you can detect that can be discussed with your DP in the morning, or at 3AM). You will be making two copies at least of the material, and preparing how and what you will shoot at least for the first couple of setups the next morning. There is a lot to do and likely you will di a good amount of it, but if it can be delegated, plan and delegate.

I lived in a small studio apartment in Manhattan when I shot Double Riddle. I had to make room in my closet for everybody, My bed was a working table, storage and nap taking spot. I slept on the couch during production. I had talked to the landlord so we could use a room in the basement next to the boilers, as a changing and waiting room. And I had talked to them about an empty apartment they had vacant on a different floor as a plan B or C. It won't hurt if you know what to do on the spot if plan A is not working.

Be smart about the neighbors. Be aware of your surroundings and show respect. If you are not ruining somebody sleep, they actually want to help you make your film in any way they can. They know you are crazy and lost case, and they will want to help you.

Set rules for yourself with the same intensity you set rules for the team. Leave your phone with your AD or check only when you are expecting an important message. Remind yourself of the effort everyone is doing and keep a very clear picture – as clear as you can – of what the story is about and how the environment you create on set adds or takes away from the work of the actors and the overall success of a particular scene.

2. PREPARATION ALLOWS FOCUS

This is self-explanatory. And my believe is that if you have done the first steps of your production responsibly, by the time you get to the set on day one you can't help but to be focused and almost in trance.

But it's worth stressing that preparation will make it easier to focus on what is important, and that is, what will be on the frame. The actors position, the light, the objects in the background, the balance of colors, the composition, the emotion, the continuity with the shot before and after, etc. It can be hard to remember all of these things on every single shot, but you have to try to make it part of that autopilot program in your brain, and the best hack I can think of, is preparing everything else so your focus is where it needs to be.

3. EXPERIMENT AND GO WITH THE FLOW

Rather, know when to go with the flow, and know when to be the flow. There is something called improvement by elimination. For example if you want to find the cure for Diabetes, do you invest 1 trillion dollars on research facilities and programs? What if you eliminate a percentage of sugar in all food instead with the same amount of money?

Every director I know of, have different strategies, but I'd like to think that directing your first film by elimination can be a valuable strategy. Eliminate paradigms. Eliminate meaningless dialogue, eliminate useless sequences. Be a curator, getting rid of things and ideas until all there is, is essential for the scene to work, can be better than adding things while trying to get something good out of it.

This or any other strategy from a book is just something for one to keep in the back of the head. That said, be flexible. If you are working with a good DP their gut may solve a problem you don't even knew you had on a particular shot. It happened a couple of times to me and the film was better because of it.

Sometimes it takes 2 minutes to try to shoot something in a way that you didn't see before, but one that could give you something special in the cutting room. And anyone on set can come up with such an idea.

Example, you have covered two actors having a conversation. Each medium shot, a wide establishing shot and maybe a close up. Lights are set, sound is rolling and the actors are now in the flow. Do one extra take and move the camera. Try a different angle. That may be the take that makes the scene works.

How and when you move the camera varies. It depends on the scene, but I find that for every scene, there is a way a camera could move from its more "obvious" position. Once again, in the context of making your first film, try something different before moving on to the next setup if you have the luxury of time. If fact, make a habit of asking yourself before you move on to the next setup, every time, how would I shoot this if I was Hitchcock? (or whoever you want).

3. DIRECTING ACTORS

The same ideas of flow, experimentation and elimination apply for performance. I have one philosophy when it comes to actors, and that is that my job is to make them look good. I don't believe in bad actors, I believe first in poor directing, only then in bad acting. Most of the directing actors' job you must have already done in the auditioning process. If you cast well, you are simply letting your actors do their job and be there to just help them keep their instrument tuned to the project you are working on.

When you audition and maybe meet with actors more than once, reading the lines with your actors as many times as possible can be useful. Listening to their voice and how they talk – what kind of character comes to mind when they speak? Is the character in the voice or not? You can run scenes with partners you are trying to match and have them read using different ideas, just as if you were in acting class. Sometimes doing this type of exercises opens up possibilities or makes everyone be on the same page of what the scene is about and how it plays best. Hopefully this will help you make final decisions.

Some directors often talk about how difficult it is to speak to actors because they don't know what to tell them, and the only and easiest way to get over it is to take an acting class. And if that's not possible, just remember that they want to please you too – assuming you know what you're doing -, so help them do that. Explain what you are looking for when it's not there, give examples and actionable directions. If your instincts are good they will help you get there. Polish together.

Every actor is different. Some actors I don't say much to, others I literally tell them where to point their eyes to and how fast to blink. Don't forget you are painting a picture, and it's your job to know how it looks like. Communicate that.

Like in a painting, things can be realistic or not. Some movies are more interesting when actors play beyond what's believable. Stanley Kubrick said this to Jack Nicholson during The Shining: "Yes, it looks real, but it's not interesting".

People can laugh when somebody dies and still be in pain, they can yell and be violent while still wanting to connect with the person in front of them, and they can whisper when they want to say something important. Humans are strange creatures. Try things and explore behavior. The actor loves play pretend and make believe. If your notes add to their work, at least they will try.

I had the blessing to work with talented actors. Even for being in the beginning of their careers, they were thoughtful, professional and connected to the material they were given. I think you have to like them and you must want them to succeed as actors while they are part of your project.

You may run across situations you did not (but could have) anticipate. And actor that seemed confident during an audition, can become insecure on set. An actor that seemed charismatic, very expressive and upbeat, could turn in a more stoic type of character, an actor that seemed more sensitive and shy can become more dominant.

The only way to avoid this is asking lots of questions to the actors about how they relate to the material and their life experience, during casting. It's not only for you to make the right call, it's also for the actor to choose working with you and play characters that they understand. But once you are on set, you must trust them, and figure things out.

If you missed the mark casting, help to build the character with more than just performance. People do things that reveal character, we all do. We use things in a particular way, or wear particular clothes, or live in a particular space. Some things may not be on the script, but if you understand the character you are building, you can work with the actor to think about how to show the world in which the character lives, and make his or her performance fit the story better.

Before blocking a scene I like to have that moment with the actors, when you just read the lines (now memorized) and we play with how the conversation sounds and how much we believe in what we are saying or not.

Here is a moment when the theory of elimination comes to play for me. I find myself often reminding actors that usually we don't act every word we say, we just say things. And when they focus on just uttering the words, their body will only do what feels natural, and I work with that. You and the actor can play between "realistic" and "interesting" in Kubrick words. A contradiction at times, but that's what makes humans complex creatures.

4. SOLVING PROBLEMS (BECAUSE YOU'LL HAVE THEM)

You don't need to have all the answers. Know this from this moment on. Being a director means you should be able to come up with an answer, but not necessarily THE answer to a problem in front of you. I don't think it is good practice to be asking everybody for an opinion all the time, but it is wise to know when, who and how in particular situations. As the saying goes, leave your ego at the door. There are a number of capable artists right there on set with ideas and it is foolish not to listen and curate those ideas when the answer in your head for whatever reason doesn't feel right.

This will always work to your benefit and for the project's benefit in the moment and later on. In the micro-culture that is created in the process of making a film, feel-good moments build trust, self-confidence and a team attitude. In one moment an idea from a gaffer that is acknowledged and implemented, means that when things go wrong, some actor forgets his or her wardrobe and everyone is busy, that gaffer who now understands his ownership of the project, will go out of his way to offer solutions or go get what's needed.

This is not to say you create those moments expecting something in return, it means that's just how life works and if you understand that, you will take advantage of it. Instead of feeling that your authority is threatened by somebody's opinion, what you will see is an opportunity to empower people, get the best ideas on the screen and strengthen the project as a whole.

Even a small production could have it's own measure of conflict. The important lesson I can share is that as a director, everything begins and ends with you. You have that power. If conflict arises, you can feed it, or extinguish it pretty quickly. Keep your cool.

An actor calls at noon to let you know he won't show up, and half of the day was planned and schedule to shoot scenes for this important character in the story. You hear to the voicemail, what do you do?

Know your story so well that like a jazz musician, you can improvise and keep the music coming. You realize the scene is important, which means you did something right by keeping it on the script. You must shoot something, but other actors for other scenes are not there, and you can't afford not shooting, it's expensive to stop an ultra low budget production.

You apply another one of life's natural laws: You do the best you can, where you are, with what you have.

Exactly that situation happened to us. One of the two actors cancelled and I lost a character just like that. I knew the lines, and Jon, the boom operator, had a jacket with a hoodie that could hide my face, and we had a dark looking basement in the building. So a scene I wrote for a restaurant, became an obscure scene with a hooded man in a basement that I could later dubbed with any voice I needed to. And the reason why I thought it would work is because I knew that the content of the scene was mysterious and dark by nature, and we were there to experiment. Problem solved, and right or wrong, the train kept moving forward.

This changed the tone of the story, but we kept going. And just like that, no matter what would come across, the attitude was to find solutions to problems, and if a better idea wouldn't come up within 5 or 10 minutes of meditation, we would just go with that solution all the way.

Other random conflicts may also arise as well in the administrative side of things. A friend of mine told me a story about his second to last night of shooting. Close to midnight; someone approached him to discuss their payment agreement. In the large scheme of life and things, it was an insignificant event; but small things like that at the wrong moment, not handled, could ruin your production unless you take quick and definite action. The lesson for him: pay your interns with more than cab rides, food, work experience and books. When somebody is working 12 hours a day for 5 days on your little movie, feeding you and being asked for all kinds of random tasks, you are not exactly doing them a favor. Whoever asked him for money, deserved it, it was just not the right time.

The elimination strategy can also help you avoid problems. We did not have an art director, makeup, or wardrobe and only used one light. That alone eliminated hundreds of potential issues related to those departments. It compromises what you can do of course, but in the context of your first film and limited resources, it plays to your advantage. In other words, sometimes avoiding sources of problems ahead of time is easier than solving them.

•

"…ANYONE WHO HAS EVER BEEN
PRIVILEDGED TO DIRECT A FILM ALSO
KNOWS, THAT ALTHOUGH IT CAN BE LIKE
TRYING TO WRITE WAR AND PEACE ON A
BUMPING CAR IN AN AMUSEMENT PARK,
WHEN YOU FINALLY GET IT RIGHT, THERE
ARE NOT MANY JOYS IN LIFE THAT CAN
EQUAL THE FEELING."

STANLEY KUBRICK

•

MAKING "DOUBLE RIDDLE, WHAT COLOR DO YOU SEE?"

1. STORY AND IDEAS

The truth is, I didn't know what story I wanted to tell, I just wanted to make a movie. That was my mindset. Over the years I had collected several ideas for stories. I even had a script almost completed, but it was impossible to think that I could produce it with the money and time goals I had imposed to myself. So I had to sit down, accept that I had 3 days to write and go with it.

I followed the steps I described in the previous chapters, looked around to what I had access to, the things that where happening in my life, and turned all of that into a story, a very simple, clichéd if you want kind of story, with my own personal touch to it.

One night, during the writing process, I met someone who read the script I was working on, and suggested I should be writing about the breakup I had just gone through. So later I did that to see what would happen, and many pages and ideas started to come up on paper because I knew all the things I was talking about. It was more a matter of turning them into fiction, add more drama, shuffle the facts with the imagined scenarios and just use that as a springboard.

At that point, I decided that if the film was a learning exercise, I didn't have to marry to a specific tone or genre. I began to write each scene as a possibility to test an idea. The opening scene was a metaphor, a man looking through a telescope (because I owned one of course). The next scene was action without words, the man comes home, and covers his girlfriend's feet, protecting her from the cold. In the background, we hear "Being There" by Hal Ashby, coming from the t.v. These three elements had something to do with the story. The movie playing said something about some of the themes I was interested in at the time. Some scenes were comic, some suspenseful, some more melodramatic, some romantic, others darker. I was trying to explore different things, and the compromise is that there was not a genre to go to by default everytime I was looking for an answer.

It was only in the editing that I decided to edit in a way that it would make it easier to describe as a noir psychological thriller, just to be able to give it a label and tell festivals what kind of movie it was. I still think this is not the right thing to do, making decisions based on the festivals' requirements, but I took that route.

To make things easier, I also used as much as I had around me in the story. I had many architecture books at home, access to blueprints, and pencils and rulers... it was easier to make the character an architect than anything else, so I used that. The other characters where "career neutral".

The plot idea for the movie didn't come in one single wave. It came in pieces and I just stitched them together. I think I was going back home in the train thinking non-stop about it when the overall concept came to mind, I could almost see the entire plot in a second. And that became the thing. You will need to watch the film to understand what I mean.

The idea of the two color pencils came up in the second round of shooting, and it wasn't even in the original script. What happened was that since I had to reduce the number of pages to keep only a few I could shoot in 4 days, I decided that I wanted a metaphor that would explain Frank's obsession with the things he was searching about, without using too much exposition in the dialogues or even the visuals. This allowed me to kill several pages of dialogues that explained the mysterious box at the beginning and what the two men were doing to Frank towards the end.

That was an idea that had nothing to do with reality –
at least not consciously -, it was just one idea I added
to the story because I wanted to try something
different.

Other times ideas came directly from the sources of
inspiration. Frank's brown jacket was from Travis
Bickle's jacket in Taxi Driver. Iris's hat was mostly
from Last Tango In Paris. Sometimes ideas of
dialogue also came from other films, like Network –
"I'm going mad as hell, and I'm not going to take it
anymore", In The Waterfront "You don't understand,
I could have been somebody, not a bum, which is
what I am, let's face it" and Scarface "…see if it
fits". Those lines have some musicality to it.
Something not necessarily explored here because it
can become too subjective, but when think of
dialogue, I'm also thinking if it just sounds good.
Almost like writing a song.

2. WRITING THE SCRIPT

I wrote, structured, and conceptualized all at the
same time. It was a mess, but I really think that's the
only way you can move forward. Let it be confusing,
let it be bad until it's better. Hammer, hammer,
hammer. The first draft of this book looked nothing
like what you are reading now; believe it or not… I

had to work very hard to write a few coherent paragraphs every now and then.

I used a working title, so I didn't even thought of a title, which is one of those things that are a waste of time. You know it will have a title, but what you really need is a story that can make for a good movie, at least potentially. Since I was living on 85th street at the time, the film was called 85th Street.

I wrote up until the night before the shoot and never stopped changing things. And as I said before, in the pause between the first round of shooting and the second, I re-wrote scenes and even came up with complete new sequences and plot points. Don't panic about not having things figured out, nobody does, or ever will.

Although movies are my main source of inspiration, a couple of books came across my journey and helped me make sense of a few things like structure and character arcs and so on. The Hero's Journey by Joseph Campbell, Making Movies by Sydney Lumet, and In The Blink of an Eye, by Walter Murch. Three very simple books that can make a difference if you are starting from zero.

3. BUILDING A TEAM

The team is probably the most important part of any project, but it also takes some trust in fate when you work fast. You hope for the best and keep getting people on board as you can.

Your first impulse will be to talk to your friends, so they can help you get your film made. In theory, they will be on board, until they're not. "If you could shoot in January it would be easier for me to help you", "right now I'm finishing this project, I could help you for a couple of hours", "Let me know when you have dates, have you considered a short film? I can definitely commit to a short film" and of course "I don't know if I can help for that budget"…

It's tough. They were genuinely busy, and bills are a real thing, yet you must keep on going. For 5 days or so, I emailed probably 100 or so random people in the different crew positions to make it all come together. These days in a city like New York, you really can have an amazing team in 48 hours posting an ad online in any of the different public platforms and services.

The best story that proves this fact was how Alex Koo, the cinematographer for Double Riddle, came on board. After doing my schedule and going for it step by step with the – don't stop no matter what – rule, I found my self with a script, actors, locations, a fridge stacked of food, a sound guy, an assistant, an intern, a gaffer, a call sheet for 8AM the next morning and still no camera or camera operator confirmed. I was not freaking out, I was just focused and working every hour of the day, emailing people and talking on the phone to be ready in the morning. Looking back, I enjoyed the energy of getting a lot done so fast. And also, that was kind of stupid.

My friends couldn't make it. I had tried friends of friends, they couldn't do it for the budget. I had tried Craigslist and I was drowned with 100 emails overnight of very talented people, but between schedule conflicts, budgets, locations, gear or just artistic affinity, nothing got confirmed. At around 9pm the night before call time, I got on the phone with Alex, after a few emails back and forth. He had asked me for a shot list via email first, and I didn't have one completely ready. So for 4 or so hours all I did was put together a shot list of the first 4 days or something like that and sent it to him before the call. I explained the project, he paused for a second, asked a few more questions, - probably thinking I was crazy - I had the answers and he said, OK, see you in the morning.

Less than 12 hours before the shoot had begun, I had no camera or camera operator, life kept asking, do you really want to do this? And I kept saying yes. I wonder if life was really trying to protect me from getting into it, but what the hell.

Connecting with my AD (assistant director) wasn't all that different but it happened 3 days or so before the shoot, what a luxury. From the behind camera crew, the AD really is the one role you don't want to make a mistake with.

He or she will be (or needs to be) both a motivational speaker and a tyrant at the same time, command and compassion. If the AD gets lost or can't communicate on set, the ship's sail will go in any direction the wind blows, and from there it can ruin the production.

I had the pleasure to come across a young filmmaker named Grace Kim. Grace responded to an ad for the job and only 72 hours or so before the shoot we met to go through the project schedule, vision and basic logistics and she helped me structure each day in what we thought was the most efficient way possible to make things happen.

The rest of the crew came through friends and people I had worked with in the past, all of them very talented and hard working. The final crew consisted of 6 people, and for a few days I had to call in back ups if one of the assistants had schedule conflicts.

Although it may sound a little esoteric, trust that the right people will find their way to the project, expect the best from them and as it happen on our shoot, things will work out.

4. FINDING ACTORS, OR FINDING CHARACTERS

Finding actors is easy in a city like New York, the challenge is finding the characters you need. If you know the characters you have written about, you want to find the right actors to play them. If any actor is able to play your character, chances are your character is not interesting enough, or doesn't have much to make it relevant to the story.

Take a moment to write down who each character is, what kind of person they are and the state of mind they find themselves in during the story. Then go find the actors that can do that.

I based my criteria for the actors thinking on their emotional peaks. I selected the scenes I thought were more dramatic, and used them for my readings. Once again I must have talked with a few hundred people online, and then auditioned 30 or 40 to find 6 to be part of the project. Those I had the chance to get to read twice, I did. And overall I did learn a few things.

You'll have an easier time if you like the actors not only for their talent but for who they are and how you get along. I tried to go intuitively with a mix of talent and easy going personalities. I will keep insisting this is in the context of your first film, where you don't have a lot of time or resources to do an extensive research.

I enjoyed all the auditions with the actors that ended up in the film and from all I learned a lot. For example, if a character will have different scenes, both dark and violent, and romantic or something like that, you should try the different scenes with the lead actors and get a good sense of their behavior in all the key aspects of the story so you have more time to work the things that go against the actors instinct. For frank I saw many actors, Including Ryan Ruby, Armand Lane and Mike Greca. They were all first options for the role and at the end schedule, age and the need of good actors in all roles, things ended up the way they did and they all did great. Mike and Martina were learning pages of dialogue daily and in his case, he also had to go form stable to unstable, from caring to losing his mind or getting a gun, from heartbreak to nightmares, one day to the next. It was challenging.

Some auditions where fun. With Iris, played by Martina Karra, we had two readings. During her second audition Martina came in crying, and I still don't know if she was playing the scene from the moment she walked in the room or what was going on, but seeing her in a way I didn't expect made me give her the role just a couple of hours after and I made no mistake.

Joe, played by Paul Foster, was the easiest part to cast. He was Joe. Sometimes it just happens that way.

The other characters where coincidences, or intuition. For Conrad, played by Michael Mulhearn, I was looking for archetypes. A white powerful older man that could stay quiet and still command respect, with some darkness to it. Michael, full of life as he is, had the ability to play also a more sinister looking guy, and that was all I needed.

The first time Michael was schedule to be on set, he a had to cancel last minute, worried about his SAG status and his ability to be in my non-sag production. That day, I had to re-write his part, get a coat with a hoodie from a crew member, and play myself a new character in the movie. That's how and why that happened. I could not afford a day of not shooting anything.

For the second phase of the shoot a couple of months later, Michael had called me to explain the situation and I still wanted him in the picture, and I re-wrote a few pages so that both his character and mine could co-exist in the story, and we worked things out. That was a lot of fun to make happen, and I wish his character have had more screen minutes to play with.

Sarah, played by Annastasia Krainik, was the archetype of a beautiful girlfriend you don't want to loose. I saw a tape of Annastasia and kept it for several weeks, but I always knew she was the one for the role. She had a strong personality, but she really is in control of her instrument and can play different emotions. This character was important in ways that other character's were not. She was the reason for Frank's downfall, so her mood, voice, tone, rhythm and words were key to make the story work dramatically. This is a good reminder that no character is an instrument on its own but rather part of an orchestra, and your job is to get out of each the sound that makes everything else works. All the work I did with her, short as it was, had to do with how we wanted Frank to come across so that things made some more sense.

The other supporting characters, played by Armand Lane (Jules), Ryan Ruby (Brian) and John Murphy

(Frank's boss), where all intuitively selected, but I was lucky all three where very versatile and I could have taken their roles to different and more dramatic places. I wish I could have developed their characters more, had I known more about their talent.

The lesson here is, don't be afraid to write small roles into the story, or short scenes that are seemingly unnecessary. If you have good actors and decent writing, I think it adds enormous "entertainment" value to the story. In that picture, each character could have easily have a couple more scenes and I think the movie could have had more to explore. I remember we did have ideas for Jules, and Conrad, and Sarah, we just never had the time to make them happen.

5. VALUE-ENGINEERING THE SCRIPT

In architecture, value-engineering is the process of simplifying a structure's configuration, design or use of materials, so as to reduce the costs of building it. Value-engineering your script to the bone every time you sit down for re-writes means you will have more room for unexpected costs and maybe, a better film.

It is easier for a production to become more expensive than less expensive. So when you write your script to be as effective as possible, as engaging as it can be, with the minimum amount of tricks, gimmicks or complex shots, the easier it will be to make it happen. Don't rely on a big explosion to make the story work. Always ask how you can achieve the same effect with less resources. Become a master of simplicity.

I always think of Richard Linklater's "Tape", written by Stephen Belber, as a great example. The entire film happens in a hotel room, and inside of it, through character, story and dialogue, Linklater, via Ethan Hawke, Uma Thurman and Robert Sean Leonard, keeps us entertained for 1 hour and 26 minutes. This film was great inspiration for me to not come up with "location excuses" when I first decided to make a movie. If you have access to a bedroom, you can make a feature film, and a good one.

Back to value-engineering; after shooting for 6 days and 3 months of editing, I realized I had a lot of footage for a 40 minute film, but with holes in the story. We didn't have the opening sequence and some of the dialogues between Michael Mulhearn (who was absent in round one) and Armand Lane. We didn't have Sarah, etc. At that point I had 30 pages of the script I had not shot, no money left and I wasn't sure it was worth finishing the project, because, as you will find, the first time you look at a rough cut, it is the worst thing you have ever seen in your entire life. And it is indeed.

But I figured I would be more frustrated in the future if I didn't finish it and used all that money and time for nothing. Here, although I'm glad I continued for the joy it brought to the actors more than anything else, if it had been for myself, I had stopped. I wasn't happy with my part of the job. But again, I went with it.

I raised some money from friends and family and we shot for 4 more days. My brother put down half of the money I needed, if you ever get to read this, thank you bud. To finish what was left in the script with the money I was able to collect (a whole 3,000 more), I knew 30 pages was too much, and watching what I had shot I could see more into the story and how things were working, and not working. So I took the script and began to pick exclusively what was needed to make some sense of the story. Entire scenes of paranoia where simplified (that hurt), and scenes with the character's father at a dinner towards the end of the picture were simply removed. I had a scene with Ryan, Paul and Mike playing basketball I really wanted to shoot, but again it had to be sacrificed. We had to value-engineer to be able to finish the story without any extras. Even after the 4 days we worked to finish, I went out alone in the snow with a small digital camera to make the snow sequence myself, weeks after we had wrapped production. Without finishing the film, I don't think I would be now able to write this book and also be better equipped to make another film in the future. You must see it that way.

In any case, spend half a day playing the movie in your head a couple of times, script at hand, and rip off the pages that don't fit, even when it hurts. Never stop optimizing.

6. EDITING & TONE

Sometime before I made Double Riddle, I had read "In The Blink of an Eye" by Walter Murch. I can't recommend this book enough to understand the work and art of editing. Storyboarding and the quality of your ideas in general –as far as movie making goes- will take another level. Editing is the most fun and the most difficult thing to do at the same time. Fun because it's during editing when you actually tell the story and make the movie become one thing or another, and hard because you have to make thousands of decisions and let go eventually, knowing it could be "just a little better" still.

Martine Scorsese said it best. If you don't feel sick after you watch the first cut of your film, something is wrong.

For Double Riddle it was about 4 months of editing, on and off. I probably came up with 5 different movies, at least two genres, and 10 different trailers in the process.

The first thing I realized when I began to put things together was that I didn't have a clear picture in my mind of what the movie should look like as a whole. The approach of experimenting on each scene, is not quite useful at the time you want the movie to be one cohesive thing instead of unrelated vignettes. So in some way I got what I set out to do. A messy, tone deaf mix of things with a main character.

Having clarity over the story, and over each scene, is different than having clarity over the movie as a whole. I think I could have made the film better had I focused for a few more hours on the movie as a whole and still explore different ideas. In other words, I should have played the entire movie in my head a few more times and see the tone of it more clearly. I don't know if it would have changed the end result dramatically but I think it would have helped knowing what to keep on the script or what to let go more easily.

For instance, I remember a friend pointing out that he would have had no day scenes outside and shoot all at night, because of the tone of the film. I wasn't going for something so dark, but the point is, I didn't even consider that option, and it was an option.

Another thing during editing is that some things will value-engineer themselves. They will not fit the picture anymore. For example, in the original script, Frank and Joe had a scene where they talked about women, and careers and Frank shared his view on why he was doing what he was doing. Joe played a few good jokes during that conversation and had some funny moments, It was a fun dialogue, but it really didn't do anything for the tone of the story, the characters or the themes I was trying to explore in the picture. It was also a long take that slowed down the pace of the movie and it was too much of a departure. That's when you remember, you wrote the whole thing in a rush and you didn't think enough about tone and how things would play in context to all the rest. And you learn.

If you combine the time I spent writing that particular scene, shooting it, editing it, etc. I could have used the same time doing another thing. The lesson here is to practice editing the movie in your head more times as part of the writing process. Interestingly enough, I also remember Grace questioning the content of that scene, and I thought it was because of the "locker room" talk of the two guys, but it wasn't just that, it was the relevance of their conversation in the story. At the end you have to choose what matters most, the scene, or the story.

7. SOUND AND MUSIC SCORING

One of the things I will approach differently next time, is all music and sound related treatment. What I did not know is that there is a difference between professional high-end sound, and the sound you need in a movie theater. If you can upgrade with a hundred bucks or so your sound equipment and/or the level of experience of the person in charge do the upgrade, cut on make up, wardrobe or eat hotdogs for a week (you, not the crew). Whatever it takes, get the best sound you can.

We live in times when the small details matter more and more. Wardrobe and make-up is not something that the entire audience will pick up on necessarily, but the sound is immediate. It's an easy and powerful way to make a difference in quality. Don't settle for good.

We did the best we could with the equipment we had, our problem wasn't talent but the noisy environments, time, and the equipment to work around it. And although we got decent sound, as I went on to use other mixers and work on other projects, I realized how much better we could have done. If it wasn't for the experience and talent of Jon and then a sound mixer in Ukraine named Vladimir

Krstic, we would have probably ended up with something not even good enough to go to a festival.

Then came music, which is also the kind of thing I can work on for hours and forget it's time for breakfast 18 hours later. You think you know music matters, but only until you are doing it with your movie you understand how true it is. I didn't have as eclectic a soundtrack as I wanted but considering most of the music was off the shelf from online libraries and very inexpensive, it is really amazing what you can do these days.

On my first cut and trailers I had used famous bands and songs I liked. I had The Doors, The Rolling Stones, Brahms and even John Cage and so on. I was having a blast. But to make that happen in reality I needed more budget than the entire post-production budget to be just for music. So I had to settle for what was available for free or low cost. Looking back, being a better writer would fix the necessity of a great score, but then again, what would be of Goodfellas or 2001 A Space Oddissey, or any Hitchcock picture, or any Chaplin film if it didn't have the scores they did. The power of great new or existing music is undeniable when you know how to use it, and that's that.

8. COLOR CORRECTING

Color correcting was in similar ways like music. Each direction affects the tone and the feeling of the story. The good news is that an audience is less sensitive to the color of the film (at least consciously) than it will be to the sound. The bad news is that as I worked on color by myself, I learned that there is a reason why colorists exist, and you should make room to collaborate with one if you can.

Find films with the look you want in your film and keep printed frames of it. Notice the colors being used. Find your palette. Take pictures of your locations, your actors and see if there is a pattern already that you can follow with the least amount of cost. If you can work with what you have and just tweak things around to give the story consistency in design and color, you can really make a difference.

To think about these things ahead of time is free, making choices on set becomes easier and the result is higher production value, and a lot more learned at the end of your film.

In short, do the color correction at the beginning, by making color conscious decisions, and polish at the end to accentuate what you need. Don't forget that between making a film, or making a painting, there is not a lot of difference, your painting just happens to move.

In Double Riddle I wanted things to have a blue cold tone, and I kept leaning towards colors matching the actors, Martina, Mike and Annastasia, all sort of blond, white and light eyed; so I would look for yellows and browns on their wardrobe whenever I could. Non of this is right or wrong, but possible ways to make decisions and "color correct" from the beginning.

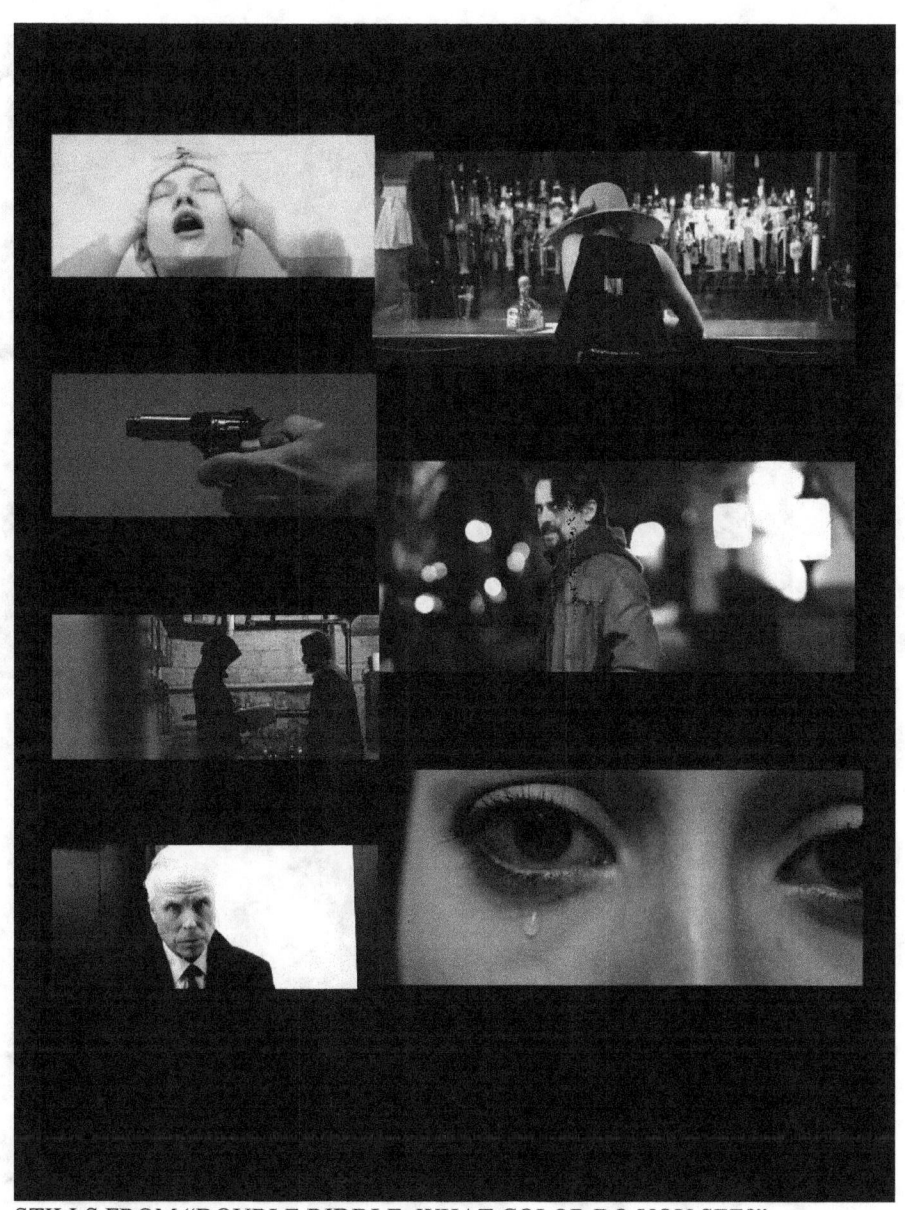

STILLS FROM "DOUBLE RIDDLE, WHAT COLOR DO YOU SEE?"

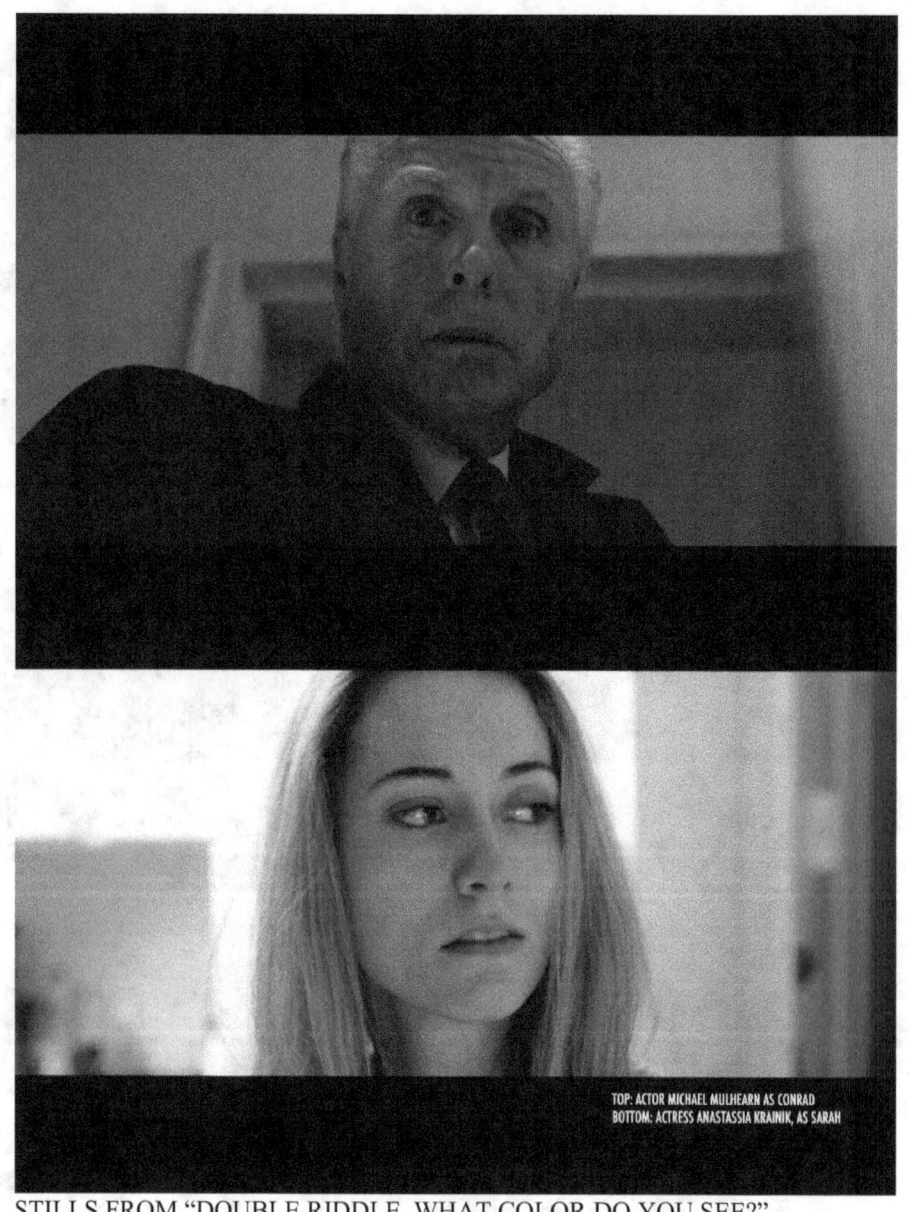

TOP: ACTOR MICHAEL MULHEARN AS CONRAD
BOTTOM: ACTRESS ANASTASSIA KRAJNIK, AS SARAH

STILLS FROM "DOUBLE RIDDLE, WHAT COLOR DO YOU SEE?"

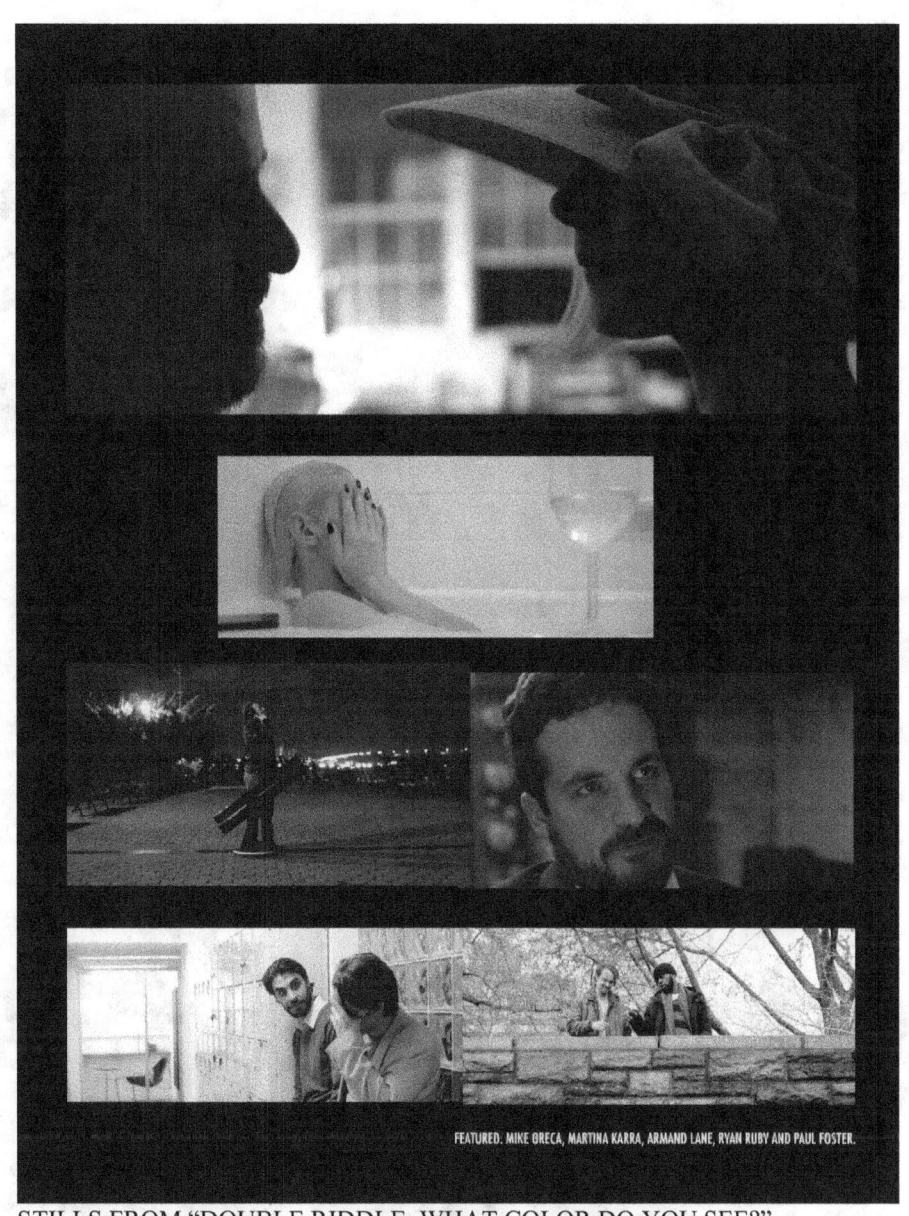

FEATURED. MIKE GRECA, MARTINA KARRA, ARMAND LANE, RYAN RUBY AND PAUL FOSTER.

STILLS FROM "DOUBLE RIDDLE, WHAT COLOR DO YOU SEE?"

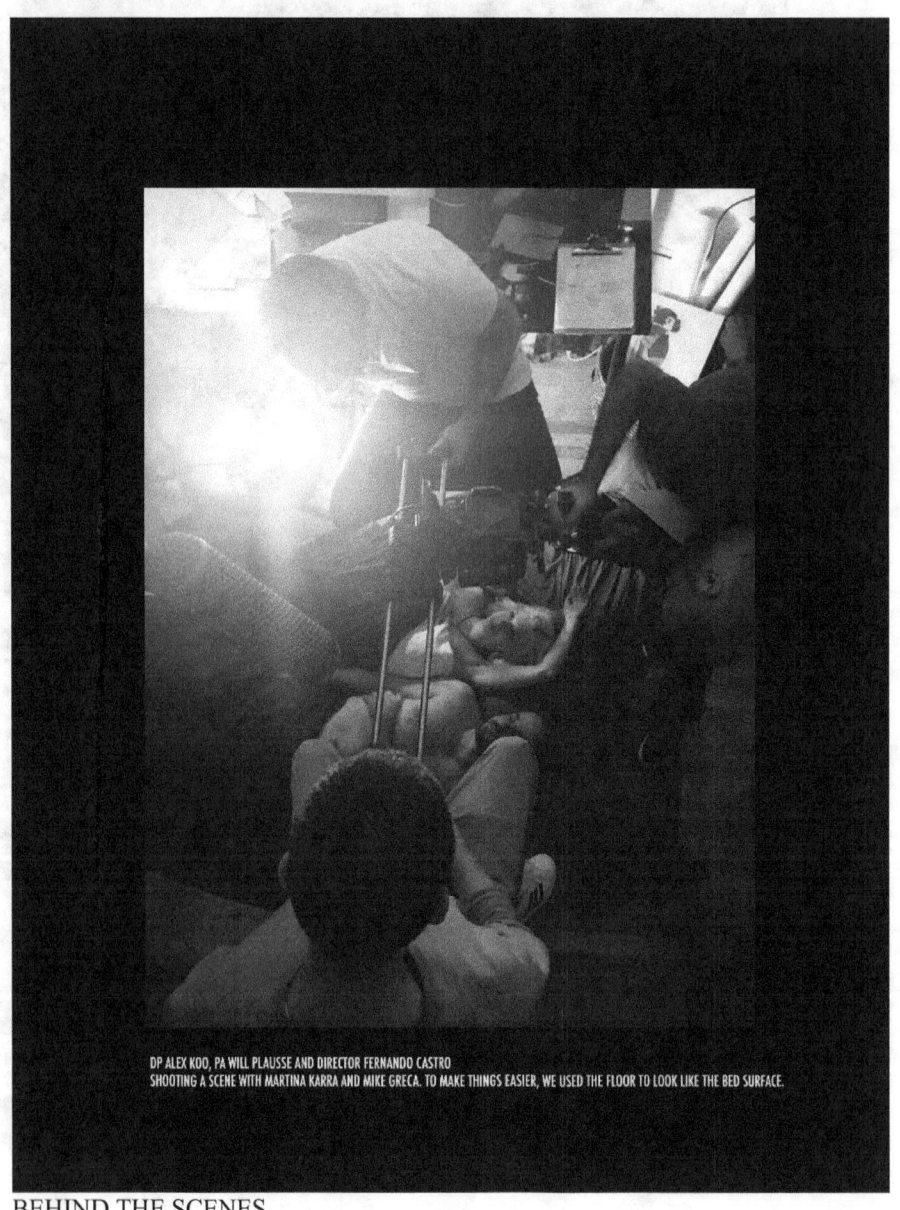

DP ALEX KOO, PA WILL PLAUSSE AND DIRECTOR FERNANDO CASTRO
SHOOTING A SCENE WITH MARTINA KARRA AND MIKE GRECA. TO MAKE THINGS EASIER, WE USED THE FLOOR TO LOOK LIKE THE BED SURFACE.

BEHIND THE SCENES

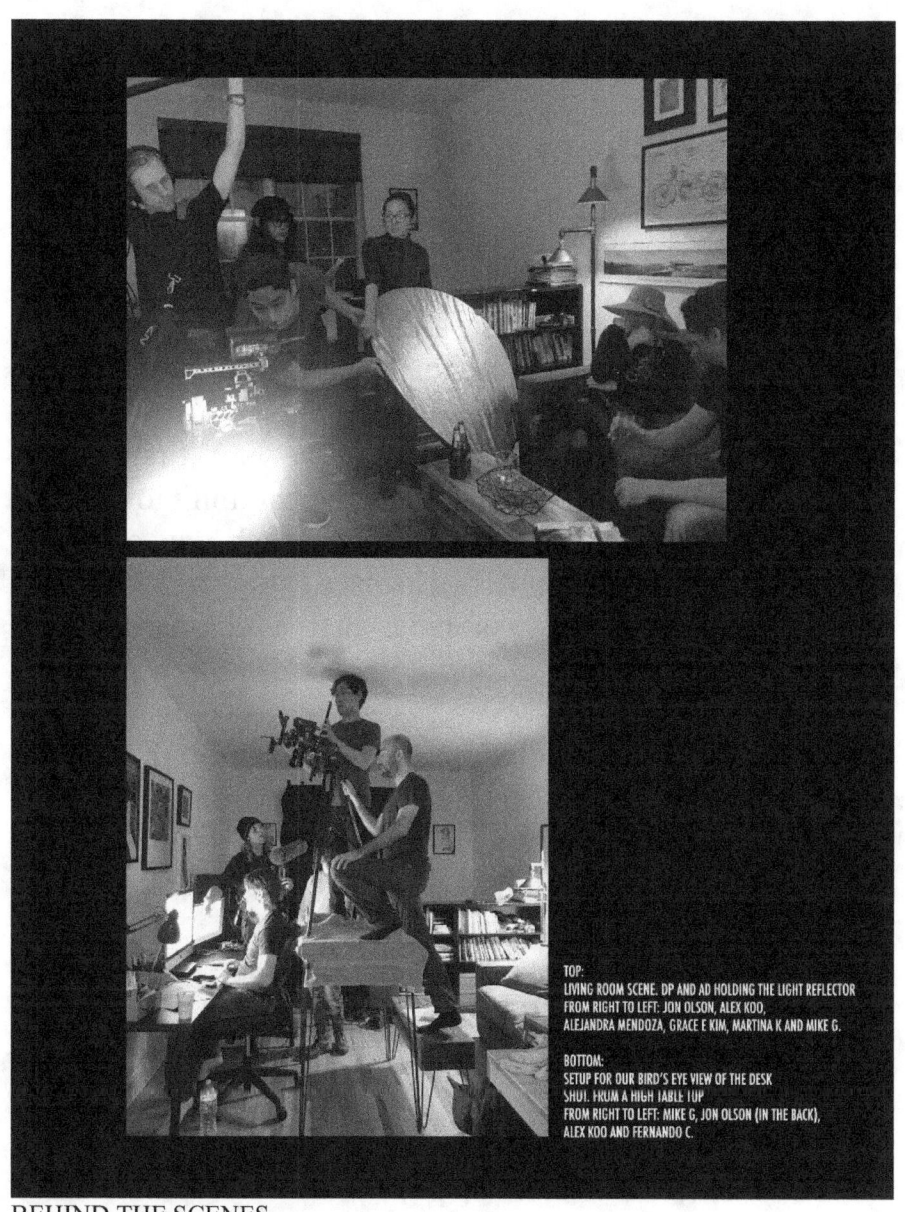

TOP:
LIVING ROOM SCENE. DP AND AD HOLDING THE LIGHT REFLECTOR
FROM RIGHT TO LEFT: JON OLSON, ALEX KOO,
ALEJANDRA MENDOZA, GRACE E KIM, MARTINA K AND MIKE G.

BOTTOM:
SETUP FOR OUR BIRD'S EYE VIEW OF THE DESK
SHOT. FROM A HIGH TABLE TOP
FROM RIGHT TO LEFT: MIKE G, JON OLSON (IN THE BACK),
ALEX KOO AND FERNANDO C.

BEHIND THE SCENES

III. AFTER

10 LESSONS LEARNED

1. Anyone can make a movie. The question is how good can it be, and if it will work dramatically speaking. The more you study films, the higher the chance to succeed.

2. Mindset is the key to see your first project through. Moving ahead has nothing to do with skill, but philosophy. For each day of work, you will find 10 reasons to stop, and 1 to keep going. Always have that 1 reason to keep going very clear.

3. Always including a topic, idea or theme you feel very strongly about in the story, will give you one powerful reason to stand by the project until it is completed.

4. Every part of the project that you elevate, elevates all the other parts. Always push quality.

5. Preparation is 80% of the task. The more you prepare, the easier it is to be flexible on set and solve any problem.

6. Most things that do not work structurally on the screenplay, will not work on the editing room. Study structure. A screenplay is a machine.

7. Casting is a turning point. Take your time to know your actors well in relation to the material you are giving them, and don't forget you will always know more than the audience, so balance your decisions with that in mind.

8. Take more risk. How you look at things, changes what you think about them. The position of a camera dictates how your audience look at things. And how you lit them also affects how they feel. Experiment more than you feel comfortable with in those two arenas.

9. How well you treat your cast and crew from beginning to end, is how they will treat your project. Common sense, or the law of reciprocity, applies in life and in making movies alike.

10 . Time is your most valuable resource, and it is because films can take so much of your life's time that you ought to love the process more so than the result. Do the best job you can. How good the work is will always be subjective to the times we are living in and the environment where your audience lives. So set that simple goal for yourself: finish it. Trust this is what you are supposed to be doing, enjoy the journey and finish the goddamn thing.

ACKNOWLEDGEMENTS

I would have not been able to write this book, had I not made my first film. And that would have not happened without the support of family, friends and colleagues who contributed to the project one way or another, to all of them my deepest thank you. Dad, Alejandro, Eliana, Nelson and Carolina. And all the friends who helped fund the production of the film. Rafi B, Cesar G, Marco and Giulia L, Juan Pablo P, Philo and Madely C, Carlos A, Glenn and Sylvia, Roberto and Connie, Monica and Renato, Alex and Lauren, David J, José V, Santiago H, Niko K, Fabio O, Eliana U, Lina A, Monica M, Flavia C, John and Vicky, Roxy and Fyad, Luis and Marcela, Haley C, Christian and Catalina, Yoly, Juan Diego B, Juan Y, Juan M, Andres B, Kiko V, Giuseppe M, Tiago and Rossana, Gianina and Cesar, and Lauren W.

Thank you to the cast and crew of Double Riddle, I wish to see your careers ascend to the heights were they belong. Alexander Koo, Grace E Kim, Jon Olson, Raghu RGV, Vencent Marfo, Alejandra Mendoza, Will Plausse, Vladimir Krstic, Mike Greca, Martina Karra, Anastassia Krainik, Armand Lane, Paul Foster, John Murphy, Ryan Ruby, and Michael Mulhearn.

To a few of my film heroes, A.Hitchcock, C.Chaplin, A.Kurasawa, J.Ozu, F.Fellini, V.De Sica, M.Antonioni, F.Truffaut, M.Ophuls, I.Bergman, A.Tarkovsky, J.Ford, B.Wilder, D.Lean, S.Leone, M.Scorsese, G.Lucas, S.Spielberg, B.DePalma, F.Coppola, A.Jodorowski, L.Buñuel, R.Polanski, S.Lumet, R.Altman, H.Ashby, W.Wenders, R.Fassbinder, J&E.Cohen, C.Nolan, T.Burton, Q.Tarantino, PT.Anderson, J.Cameron, D.Lynch, R.Linklater, D.Fincher, A.Payne, J.Woo, W.Kar Wai, A.Iñarritu, G.DelToro, A.Cuarón, and S.Kubrick, and all who are talented and lucky enough to get it right at least once, thank you for your madness.

And to the one who got me inspired to do all of this to begin with, wherever you may be when you read this, IMV.

New York, October 25th, 2019

www.ingramcontent.com/pod-product-compliance
Lightning Source LLC
Chambersburg PA
CBHW081518220526
45467CB00010B/2966